Wordly Wise

Book B

Kenneth Hodkinson

Educators Publishing Service, Inc.

Cambridge and Toronto

Introduction to Wordly Wise A, B, and C

The *Wordly Wise ABC* series of vocabulary books helps students to think not only about words and how we define them but also about the world of things and ideas for which words are referents.

A student may "know" what an elephant is, but how would she or he define *elephant*? Book A offers a definition of the word that is sufficiently broad to encompass both the Indian and African varieties; it follows this with an illustrative sentence that explains the ways in which the two types differ; it also includes a drawing that shows these differences.

Eight to twelve words are covered in each lesson in similar fashion. Some of these words the student will "know"; some he or she will not know. For some words, one meaning may be known but not other, less common, meanings.

Every vocabulary word in Book A has an accompanying picture (a nonverbal definition). The frequency of pictures in relation to the text is reduced from Book A to B and from B to C.

All three books in the *ABC* series test and reinforce the student's understanding of the meanings of the words on the Word List in a True/False exercise. Here the student is required to discriminate between a correct (True) and an incorrect (False) definition for each meaning of each word.

After this comes a Hidden Message puzzle that challenges the student to find the answer to a riddle by matching definitions with words from the Word List.

Then comes a Crossword Puzzle; the clues are illustrative sentences (different from those on the Word List pages) with one word, taken from the Word List, missing. This word, if correctly chosen, fits the puzzle. Book A has an additional feature, a set of pictorial clues incorporated into the crossword diagram.

Book C has an additional exercise in which the student replaces a cumbersome phrase with a single word from the Word List. This prepares the student for Book 1 of the *Wordly Wise* Books 1–9 series. The definitions and illustrative sentences are confined to a single page of dictionary format to accommodate this additional exercise, and the crossword puzzles in Book C appear as review exercises after two lessons. (In Book 1, crossword puzzles appear after every three lessons.)

Illustrations by Dana Franzen.

EDUCATORS PUBLISHING SERVICES, INC.
31 Smith Place, Cambridge, MA 02138

April 2001 Printing

WORD LIST

ache (6)*
angle (10)
ape (4)
award (8)

badge (7)
barrel (1)
batch (1)
beach (10)
boulder (8)
brake (3)
branch (9)
brooch (9)
brush (9)

calendar (1)
casual (8)
center (6)
cereal (10)
chapter (4)
chest (9)
child (5)
chores (4)
churn (8)
climb (2)
comfort (7)
corner (6)
crack (9)
cradle (10)
croak (5)
cry (9)

dart (1)
deadly (8)
diet (4)
dough (5)
dozen (5)
drama (3)

echo (8)
embroider (10)
errand (8)

fang (10)
feather (7)
frigid (10)

girder (8)

hood (5)

icicle (6)
igloo (6)
inch (2)

kneel (2)
knob (2)
knot (7)
knuckle (2)

label (5)
lean (10)
letter (7)
lie (6)
lizard (2)

manhole (1)
midnight (3)

needle (2)
notch (7)

oar (5)

path (2)
picnic (2)
pint (3)

quarter (3)

ramble (6)
raw (3)
rim (6)
ripple (3)
ruler (9)

saddle (5)
satchel (1)
serpent (1)
shin (7)
skim (7)
slogan (8)
soak (9)
stare (9)
surname (4)

tackle (1)
tail (7)
trade (4)
train (4)

understand (4)

whale (3)

zigzag (5)

*Numbers in parentheses refer to the Word List in which the word appears.

1

WORD LIST 1

barrel   dart   satchel
batch   manhole   serpent
calendar   tackle

A **barrel** is a large, round container with a flat top and bottom and a middle that bulges out: *To make each barrel, workers fit curved wooden pieces together and hold them in place with round metal bands.*

The **barrel** of a gun is the long metal tube from which bullets are shot: *You aim the gun by looking along the barrel.*

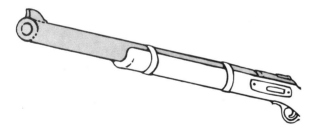

A **batch** is an amount of something handled at one time: *The first batch of cookies just came out of the oven.*

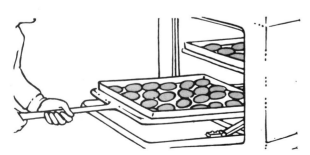

A **calendar** is a chart that shows how the year is divided into months, weeks, and days: *We wait until January 1 before putting up the new calendar.*

To **dart** is to move in a quick and sudden way: *I saw her dart across the street after the ball.*

A **dart** is a long, pointed object made to stick into whatever it is thrown at: *A dart has fins on one end to make it go straight when thrown.*

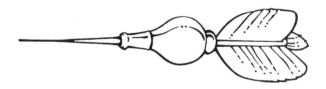

A **manhole** is a large opening in the street with a cover that can be taken off: *Workers go down the manholes to make repairs on pipes, wires, or sewers under the street.*

A **satchel** is a bag used to carry such things as books and papers: *Her satchel was bulging with books she had just taken out of the library.*

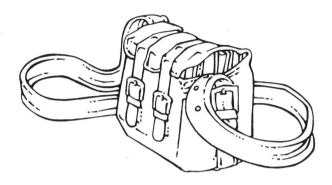

A **serpent** is a large snake: *The python is a serpent that can grow to be almost thirty feet long.*

Tackle is a collection of small tools and other bits and pieces needed to do something: *A box of fishing tackle contains hooks, lines, floats, and other things needed for fishing.*

To **tackle** is to do or to try to do something: *The roof is leaking, but we cannot tackle the job of fixing it until it stops raining.*

To **tackle** is to take on a player in a game in order to try to get the ball away: *You are not allowed to tackle anyone in the game of soccer.*

TRUE OR FALSE 1

Some of the sentences below are true and some are false. On the line to the left of each sentence, write *T* if you think the sentence is true, and *F* if you think the sentence is false.

_____ 1. A barrel is a large, round container with a flat top and bottom and a middle that bulges out.

_____ 2. A barrel of a gun is the long metal tube from which bullets are shot.

_____ 3. A batch is an amount of something handled at one time.

_____ 4. A batch is the taking on of a player in a game to get the ball away.

_____ 5. A calendar is a collection of small tools and other bits and pieces needed to do something.

_____ 6. A calendar is a chart that shows how the year is divided into months, weeks, and days.

_____ 7. A dart is a long, pointed object made to stick into whatever it is thrown at.

_____ 8. To dart is to move in a quick and sudden way.

_____ 9. A manhole is the long metal tube of a gun from which bullets are shot.

_____ 10. A manhole is a large opening in the street with a cover that can be taken off.

_____ 11. A satchel is an amount of something handled at one time.

_____ 12. A satchel is a bag used to carry books, papers, and other such things.

_____ 13. A serpent is a large snake.

_____ 14. A serpent is a move to do something.

_____ 15. To tackle is to take on a player in a game to try to get the ball away.

_____ 16. To tackle is to do or to try to do something.

Check your answers against the correct ones below. They are not in order. This is to prevent your eye from catching sight of the correct answers before you have had a chance to do the exercise on your own.

14 F.   1 T.   10 T.   7 T.   5 F.   16 T.   3 T.   12 T.
8 T.   2 T.   13 T.   15 T.   9F.   4 F.   6 T.   11 F.

4

HIDDEN MESSAGE 1

In the boxes next to each definition, write the correct vocabulary word from Word List 1. Put one letter in each box. If you do this properly, the long boxes running from top to bottom will answer the following riddle:

What did Silly Billy grow when he took up farming?

1. a large opening in the street with a cover that can be taken off

2. to do or to try to do something

3. a chart that shows how the year is divided into months, weeks, and days

4. a large, round container with a flat top and bottom and a middle that bulges out

5. to take on a player in a game to try to get the ball away

6. a long, pointed object made to stick into whatever it is thrown at

7. an amount of something handled at one time

8. a large snake

9. a bag used to carry such things as books and papers

10. to move in a quick and sudden way

11. a collection of small tools and other bits and pieces needed to do something

12. the long metal tube of a gun from which bullets are shot

CROSSWORD 1

Decide what word from Word List 1 is missing from each sentence below. For the first group of sentences (Clues Across), write each answer in the boxes running across on the puzzle on the next page. For the second group (Clues Down), write each answer in the boxes running down.

Work out the sentences in any order you like; just be sure to match the number of the sentence with the number in the box. Put only one letter in each box. If all your answers are correct, all the words on the puzzle will fit together.

Clues Across

3. Here is the last _____ of letters that need to be answered.

5. The wine is first kept in a _____, and is later poured into bottles.

6. Kirsten put the snack in her _____ between her dictionary and her math homework.

9. Justin looked at the _____ and saw that this year his birthday comes on a Saturday.

11. The most feared _____ in India is the cobra.

Clues Down

1. The old sailor got out his sewing _____ to mend the holes in his clothes.

2. After a gun has been fired, the inside of the _____ should be cleaned.

4. A railing was put around the open _____ to prevent people from falling into it.

7. Cleaning up the basement is our next job, and we will _____ it tomorrow.

8. We watched the birds _____ back and forth over the pond looking for bugs to eat.

10. The first _____ I threw hit the center of the target.

WORD LIST 2

climb	knob	needle
inch	knuckle	path
kneel	lizard	picnic

To **climb** is to move upward: *It takes skill to climb a mountain.*

An **inch** is a measure of length. Twelve inches equal one foot: *The line below is one inch long.*

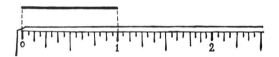

To **inch** is to move very slowly: *We watched the turtle inch its way across the road.*

To **kneel** is to go down on one or both knees: *She had to kneel down to do the weeding in her garden.*

A **knob** is a smooth, round handle that fits the hand: *We saw the knob on the door turn slowly, and we knew someone was on the other side trying to get in.*

A **knuckle** is a place on a finger where two bones are joined: *Slide the ring over your knuckle to get it off.*

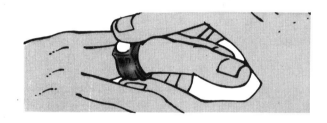

A **lizard** is an animal with a long body and tail, four legs, and scaly skin: *The chameleon (ka-me-lee-on) is a lizard that can change the color of its skin.*

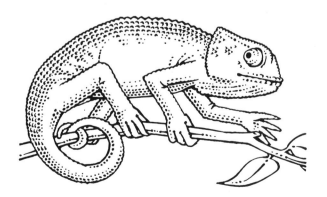

A **needle** is the small, pointed part of a record player that touches the record as it turns: *The needle on the stereo is worn out from being used so much.*

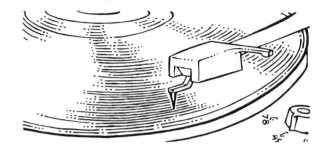

A **needle** is a long, thin, pointed leaf of a pine tree: *The needles on a pine tree do not fall off when winter comes.*

A **needle** is a long, pointed object used for sewing. It has a hole at one end that thread can be passed through: *I will thread the needle if you will sew on the button.*

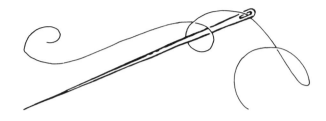

A **path** is a way that is marked out for walking: *We cleared a path through the thick snow.*

A **picnic** is a meal made to be eaten outdoors: *We will have a picnic in the park this Saturday if it is sunny.*

9

TRUE OR FALSE 2

Some of the sentences below are true and some are false. On the line to the left of each sentence, write _T_ if you think the sentence is true, and _F_ if you think the sentence is false.

_____ 1. To climb is to go down on one or both knees.

_____ 2. To climb is to move upward.

_____ 3. To inch is to move very slowly.

_____ 4. An inch is a measure of length. Twelve inches equal one foot.

_____ 5. To kneel is to go down on one knee.

_____ 6. To kneel is to go down on both knees.

_____ 7. A knob is a finger joint.

_____ 8. A knob is a smooth, round handle that fits the hand.

_____ 9. A knuckle is a long, pointed object used for sewing.

_____ 10. A knuckle is a place on a finger where two bones are joined.

_____ 11. A lizard is an animal with a long body and tail, four legs, and scaly skin.

_____ 12. A lizard is a large snake.

_____ 13. A needle is a long, thin, pointed leaf of a pine tree.

_____ 14. A needle is the small, pointed part of a record player that touches the record as it turns.

_____ 15. A path is a way that is marked out for walking.

_____ 16. A path is an amount of something handled at one time.

_____ 17. A picnic is a meal made to be eaten outdoors.

_____ 18. A picnic is a job that needs to be done.

Check your answers against the correct ones below. They are not in order. This is to prevent your eye from catching sight of the correct answers before you have had a chance to do the exercise on your own.

14 T.	7 F.	18 F.	3 T.	17 T.	10 T.	1 F.	5 T.	8 T.
16 F.	6 T.	2 T.	9 F.	12 F.	13 T.	4 T.	15 T.	11 T.

HIDDEN MESSAGE 2

In the boxes next to each definition, write the correct vocabulary word from Word List 2. Put one letter in each box. If you do this properly, the long boxes running from top to bottom will answer the following riddle:

Why does Silly Millie think that hot is faster than cold?

1. a measure of length, twelve of which equal one foot

2. a long, pointed object used for sewing

3. a place on a finger where two bones are joined

4. to go down on one or both knees

5. to move very slowly

6. an animal with a long body and tail, four legs, and scaly skin

7. a way that is marked out for walking

8. a meal made to be eaten outdoors

9. to move upward

10. a smooth, round handle that fits the hand

11. a long, thin, pointed leaf of a pine tree

12. the small, pointed part of a record player that touches the record as it turns

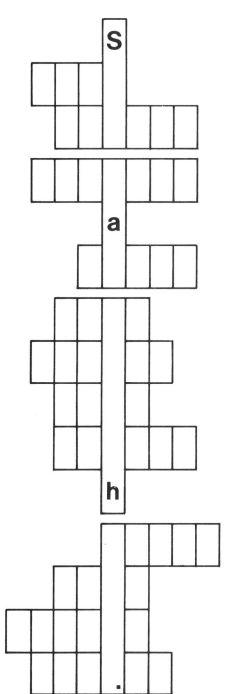

CROSSWORD 2

Decide what word from Word List 2 is missing from each sentence below. For the first group of sentences (Clues Across), write each answer in the boxes running across on the puzzle on the next page. For the second group (Clues Down), write each answer in the boxes running down.

Work out the sentences in any order you like; just be sure to match the number of the sentence with the number in the box. Put only one letter in each box. If all your answers are correct, all the words on the puzzle will fit together.

Clues Across

3. The gecko is a _____ that comes out mainly at night.

4. Sally has grown almost an _____ and a half since I last saw her.

6. _____ your way carefully along the ledge, and you won't fall off.

9. Grandpa banged on the door with his _____.

11. We watched the airplane _____ higher and higher.

12. You will need a _____ and thread to fix the rip in your jeans.

Clues Down

1. We packed a basket full of food for our _____ at the beach.

2. Follow the _____ through the woods until you reach the pond.

5. The _____ of the Scotch pine tree is longer than that of the blue spruce.

7. The _____ on this drawer is loose and needs to be screwed on tightly.

8. I cannot use my stereo until I get a new _____ for it.

10. She has to _____ to reach the books on the bottom shelf.

13

WORD LIST 3

<table>
<tr><td>brake</td><td>pint</td><td>raw</td></tr>
<tr><td>drama</td><td>quarter</td><td>ripple</td></tr>
<tr><td>midnight</td><td></td><td>whale</td></tr>
</table>

A **brake** is anything used to stop or slow down something moving by pressing, scraping, or rubbing against one of its parts: *The brake slows down the bicycle by rubbing against the wheel.*

To **brake** is to cause something that is moving to slow down or stop: *You should brake the car before you make a sharp turn.*

Drama is the activity of putting on plays: *She studied drama in college and is now a famous actress.*

A **drama** is a story written to be performed by actors and actresses: *"The Miracle Worker" is a drama that tells the story of Helen Keller.*

Midnight is twelve o'clock at night, the end of one day and the start of the next: *The old year ends at midnight on December 31.*

A **pint** is a measure equal to one half of a quart: *There are two eight-ounce cups to a pint.*

A **quarter** is one of four equal parts: *Cut the pie into quarters since there are four of you to share it.*

A **quarter** is an American coin worth twenty-five cents: *The book cost seventy-five cents, so I got a quarter in change for the dollar I gave the clerk.*

Raw means not cooked: *Raw carrots are better for you than cooked ones.*

Raw means with the skin rubbed off a part of the body: *His heel was raw because his shoe rubbed against the back of his foot as he walked.*

A **ripple** is a small wave: *The frog made a ripple on the water when it hopped into the pond.*

A **whale** is a large, air-breathing sea animal shaped like a fish: *The blue whale is the largest animal that has ever lived.*

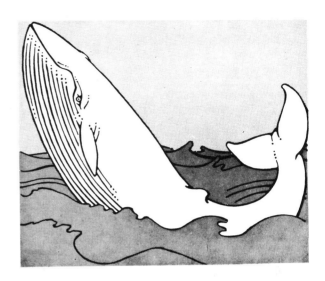

TRUE OR FALSE 3

Some of the sentences below are true and some are false. On the line to the left of each sentence, write _T_ if you think the sentence is true, and _F_ if you think the sentence is false.

_____ 1. To brake is to cause something that is moving to slow down or stop.

_____ 2. To brake is to move in a quick and sudden way.

_____ 3. Drama is the activity of putting on plays.

_____ 4. A drama is a story written to be performed by actors and actresses.

_____ 5. Midnight is the end of one day and the start of the next.

_____ 6. Midnight is twelve o'clock at night.

_____ 7. A pint is a measure equal to one half of a quart.

_____ 8. A pint is one of four equal parts of something.

_____ 9. A quarter is an American coin worth twenty-five cents.

_____ 10. A quarter is one of four equal parts of something.

_____ 11. Raw means not cooked.

_____ 12. Raw means with the skin rubbed off a part of the body.

_____ 13. A ripple is a large, air-breathing sea animal shaped like a fish.

_____ 14. A ripple is a small wave.

_____ 15. A whale is an American coin worth twenty-five cents.

_____ 16. A whale is a large, air-breathing sea animal shaped like a fish.

Check your answers against the correct ones below. They are not in order. This is to prevent your eye from catching sight of the correct answers before you have had a chance to do the exercise on your own.

11 T.   5 T.   16 T.   8 F.   1 T.   14 T.   7 T.   2 F.
15 F.   10 T.   13 F.   3 T.   12 T.   4 T.   9 T.   6 T.

HIDDEN MESSAGE 3

In the boxes next to each definition, write the correct vocabulary word from Word List 3. Put one letter in each box. If you do this properly, the long boxes running from top to bottom will answer the following riddle:

What kind of monster is easiest to keep clean?

1. anything used to stop or slow down something moving by pressing, scraping, or rubbing against one of its parts

2. not cooked

3. the activity of putting on plays

4. a large, air-breathing sea animal shaped like a fish

5. one of four equal parts

6. a measure equal to one half of a quart

7. twelve o'clock at night, the end of one day and the start of the next

8. to cause something that is moving to slow down or stop

9. a story written to be performed by actors and actresses

10. an American coin worth twenty-five cents

11. with the skin rubbed off a part of the body

12. a small wave

CROSSWORD 3

Decide what word from Word List 3 is missing from each sentence below. For the first group of sentences (Clues Across), write each answer in the boxes running across on the puzzle on the next page. For the second group (Clues Down), write each answer in the boxes running down.

Work out the sentences in any order you like; just be sure to match the number of the sentence with the number in the box. Put only one letter in each box. If all your answers are correct, all the words on the puzzle will fit together.

Clues Across

2. There was so little wind that there was hardly a _____ on the water.

5. When the clock struck _____, Cinderella ran from the ball.

8. Rosita asked me to change a _____, so I gave her a nickel and two dimes.

10. Don't _____ while riding your bike over sand, or you may skid and fall off.

12. Marcel is interested in _____ and goes often to see plays.

Clues Down

1. We watched an exciting _____ on television about a girl who was born with one arm, but who became a champion gymnast.

3. A _____ of ice cream is enough for three people.

4. A _____ has to come to the surface of the water to breathe.

6. If you two each take a _____ of the cake, then half of it will be left.

7. A car's hand _____ is used to keep the car from moving while it is parked.

9. His wrists were rubbed _____ by the straps of his new ski poles.

11. Some cats like their meat cooked, while others like it _____.

19

WORD LIST 4

ape	diet	trade
chapter	surname	train
chores		understand

An **ape** is a large, monkeylike animal without a tail. It stands almost straight and walks on two hind legs: *The largest ape is the gorilla, which grows to be over six feet tall.*

A **chapter** is any one of the main parts of a long book: *He took a break when he finished writing the first chapter of his book.*

Chores are small jobs done around a house or farm: *Tom's daily chores include feeding the pigs and hens.*

A **diet** is the food and drink usually taken by an animal or person: *Grass, hay, oats, and water make up the diet of a horse.*

A **diet** is a special choice of foods taken for health reasons: *Because of his weak heart, the doctor put him on a salt-free diet.*

To **diet** is to limit what one eats and drinks, especially to lose weight: *Since he started to diet last month, Roberto has lost ten pounds.*

A **surname** is a last name or family name: *When a woman marries, she can take her husband's surname as her own.*

A **trade** is a kind of work that calls for skill and that is often done with the hands: *I asked Marian if she had a trade, and she said she was a carpenter.*

To **trade** is to swap or exchange one thing for another: *I said I would trade my apple for her banana.*

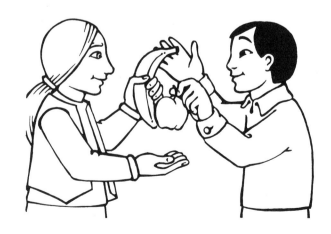

A **train** is part of a long dress that trails on the floor behind the woman wearing it: *A wedding dress usually has a long train.*

A **train** is a connected line of railroad cars that are pulled by an engine: *She was given a toy train by her Uncle Bruno for her birthday.*

To **train** is to learn or practice certain things that call for skill to be done well: *A boxer has to train very hard before each fight.*

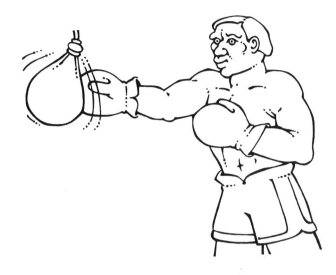

To **understand** is to get the meaning of: *Do you understand what you have just read?*

To **understand** is to know how someone else feels or thinks: *Charlie is unhappy because he believes that no one understands him.*

21

TRUE OR FALSE 4

Some of the sentences below are true and some are false. On the line to the left of each sentence, write *T* if you think the sentence is true, and *F* if you think the sentence is false.

_____ 1. An ape is any small job done around the house or farm.

_____ 2. An ape is a large, monkeylike animal without a tail. It stands almost straight and walks on two hind legs.

_____ 3. A chapter is a last name or a family name.

_____ 4. A chapter is any one of the main parts of a long book.

_____ 5. Chores are small jobs done around the house or farm.

_____ 6. Chores are special kinds of food taken for health reasons.

_____ 7. A diet is the food and drink usually taken by an animal or person.

_____ 8. A diet is special choice of foods taken for health reasons.

_____ 9. To diet is to learn or practice certain things that call for skill to be done well.

_____ 10. A surname is a last name or family name.

_____ 11. A surname is a kind of work that calls for skill and that often is done with the hands.

_____ 12. To trade is to swap or exchange one thing for another.

_____ 13. A trade is a kind of work that calls for skill and that is often done with the hands.

_____ 14. A train is a connected line of railroad cars that are pulled by an engine.

_____ 15. A train is a part of a long dress that trails on the floor behind the woman wearing it.

_____ 16. To train is to learn or practice certain things that call for skill to be done well.

_____ 17. To understand is to know how someone else feels or thinks.

_____ 18. To understand is to get the meaning of.

Check your answers against the correct ones below. They are not in order. This is to prevent your eye from catching sight of the correct answers before you have had a chance to do the exercise on your own.

6 F.	9 F.	14 T.	12 T.	2 T.	7 T.	17 T.	11 F.	1 F.
16 T.	4 T.	3 F.	18 T.	10 T.	5 T.	15 T.	8 T.	13 T.

HIDDEN MESSAGE 4

In the boxes next to each definition, write the correct vocabulary word from Word List 4. Put one letter in each box. If you do this properly, the long boxes running from top to bottom will answer the following riddle:

If Silly Billy cuts his mother's hat into five big pieces and ten small pieces, what time is it?

1. to know how someone else feels or thinks

2. a connected line of railroad cars that are pulled by an engine

3. a large, tailless, monkeylike animal that stands almost straight and walks on two hind legs

4. a part of a long dress that trails on the floor behind the woman wearing it

5. small jobs done around a house or farm

6. to limit what one eats and drinks, especially to lose weight

7. to get the meaning of

8. to swap or exchange one thing for another

9. a last or family name

10. a special choice of foods taken for health reasons

11. any one of the main parts of a long book

12. a kind of work that calls for skill and that is often done with the hands

13. to learn or practice certain things that call for skill to be done well

23

CROSSWORD 4

Decide what word from Word List 4 is missing from each sentence below. For the first group of sentences (Clues Across), write each answer in the boxes running across on the puzzle on the next page. For the second group (Clues Down), write each answer in the boxes running down.

Work out the sentences in any order you like; just be sure to match the number of the sentence with the number in the box. Put only one letter in each box. If all your answers are correct, all the words on the puzzle will fit together.

Clues Across

3. A book usually begins with _____ One.

6. If you tell your mother why you're afraid to come, I'm sure she will _____.

8. I couldn't answer the question because I didn't _____ it.

10. He will _____ for three years to become a pilot.

11. Fresh fruit and vegetables are important items in a person's _____.

12. An orangutan is a long-armed, short-legged _____ that lives in trees.

Clues Down

1. One of my evening _____ is taking out the trash.

2. I offered to _____ my catcher's mitt for his football.

4. People who don't like to travel by car or plane can take the _____.

5. His first name is Jack, and his _____ is Robinson.

7. Why did you just eat three sugar doughnuts if you're trying to _____?

9. You could be a plumber, but it takes a long time to learn that _____.

10. The queen's dress had a long _____ that was held by two pageboys when she walked.

WORD LIST 5

child	dozen	oar
croak	hood	saddle
dough	label	zigzag

A **child** is a young boy or girl: *A small child should not be left alone in the house.*

A **child** is a son or daughter of any age: *Mr. Kaplan was sad when his only child got married and moved away.*

To **croak** is to make deep, rasping or rough sounds in the throat: *Frogs croak a lot at night.*

Dough is a mixture of flour and water or milk that is used to make bread and other baked goods: *You must press and squeeze the dough for about five minutes before you shape it into loaves.*

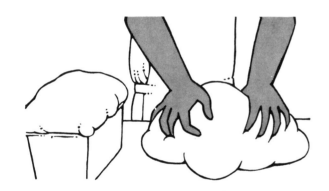

A **dozen** is a group of twelve: *Get a loaf of bread and a dozen eggs at the store.*

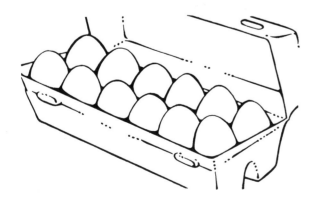

A **hood** is a head covering often fastened to the collar of a coat: *Put up your hood if it starts to snow.*

A **hood** is the part of a car that fits over the engine and that can be raised and lowered: *Be sure the hood is shut properly before you drive off.*

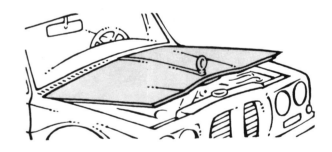

A **label** is a piece of paper or cloth that can be stuck or sewn to an object to tell something about it: *The label sewn to the inside of the coat gave the name of the store where it was bought.*

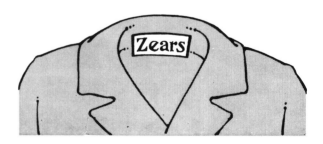

26

To **label** is to mark an object with a piece of paper or cloth to tell something about it: *I will label the jars after you put the apple jelly in them.*

An **oar** is a long pole that is flat and wide at one end. Two of them are used to row and steer a boat: *Try not to splash too much as you dip each oar in the water.*

A **saddle** is a padded leather seat that the rider of a horse sits on: *Loosen or tighten the straps that hold the saddle on the horse until it fits just right.*

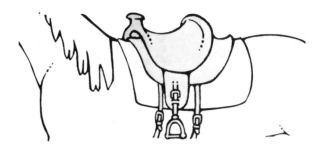

To **saddle** is to strap a seat onto a horse for riding: *We will leave as soon as they saddle the horses.*

A **zigzag** is a line that goes sharply from side to side and back again: *To make a picture of lightning, she drew a zigzag line.*

TRUE OR FALSE 5

Some of the sentences below are true and some are false. On the line to the left of each sentence, write *T* if you think the sentence is true, and *F* if you think the sentence is false.

_____ 1. A child is a young boy or girl.

_____ 2. A child is a son or daughter of any age.

_____ 3. To croak is to make deep, rasping or rough sounds in the throat.

_____ 4. To croak is to move very slowly.

_____ 5. Dough is the activity of putting on plays.

_____ 6. Dough is a mixture of flour and water or milk that is used to make bread and other baked goods.

_____ 7. A dozen is a line that goes sharply from side to side and back again.

_____ 8. A dozen is a group of twelve.

_____ 9. A hood is the part of a car that fits over the engine and that can be raised and lowered.

_____ 10. A hood is a head covering often fastened to the collar of a coat.

_____ 11. A label is a piece of paper or cloth that can be stuck or sewn to an object to tell something about it.

_____ 12. A label is a padded leather seat that the rider of a horse sits on.

_____ 13. An oar is a long pole that is flat and wide at one end. Two of them are used to row and steer a boat.

_____ 14. An oar is a small wave.

_____ 15. A saddle is a padded leather seat that the rider of a horse sits on.

_____ 16. A saddle is a place on a finger where two bones are joined.

_____ 17. A zigzag is a deep, rasping or rough sound made in the throat.

_____ 18. A zigzag is a line that goes sharply from side to side and back again.

Check your answers against the correct ones below. They are not in order. This is to prevent your eye from catching sight of the correct answers before you have had a chance to do the exercise on your own.

17 F.   2 T.   9 T.   13 T.   6 T.   10 T.   8 T.   7 F.   11 T.
3 T.   15 T.   18 T.   1 T.   14 F.   4 F.   12 F.   16 F.   5 F.

HIDDEN MESSAGE 5

In the boxes next to each definition, write the correct vocabulary word from Word List 5. Put one letter in each box. If you do this properly, the long boxes running from top to bottom will answer the following riddle:

Why did Silly Billy need an extra sock?

1. a young boy or girl

2. a piece of paper or cloth that can be stuck or sewn to an object to tell something about it

3. a line that goes sharply from side to side and back again

4. to make deep, rough or rasping sounds in the throat

5. to mark an object with a piece of paper or cloth to tell something about it

6. a padded leather seat that the rider of a horse sits on

7. a group of twelve

8. a head covering often fastened to the collar of a coat

9. a son or daughter of any age

10. to strap a seat onto a horse for riding

11. a long pole that is flat and wide at one end; two of them are used to row and steer a boat

12. a mixture of flour and water or milk that is used to make bread and other baked goods

13. the part of a car that fits over the engine and that can be raised and lowered

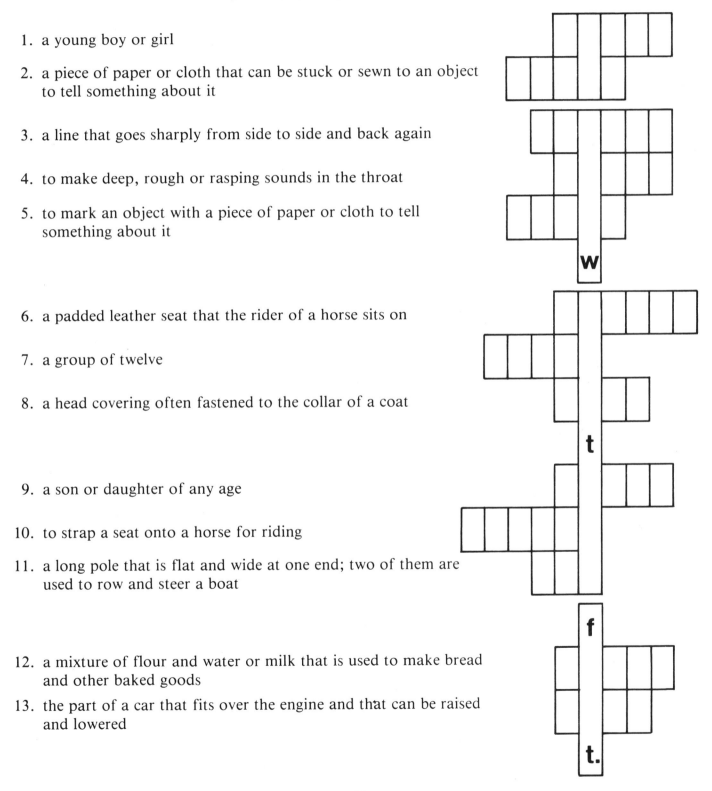

29

CROSSWORD 5

Decide what word from Word List 5 is missing from each sentence below. For the first group of sentences (Clues Across), write each answer in the boxes running across on the puzzle on the next page. For the second group (Clues Down), write each answer in the boxes running down.

Work out the sentences in any order you like; just be sure to match the number of the sentence with the number in the box. Put only one letter in each box. If all your answers are correct, all the words on the puzzle will fit together.

Clues Across

3. My ears were getting cold, so I pulled up the _____ on my jacket.

5. The _____ had come off the can, so we could not tell what was inside it.

7. If you divide a _____ oranges among six people, each person will have two.

9. The man at the gas station lifted the _____ to check the oil.

10. Keep adding flour a little at a time until the _____ is no longer sticky.

12. The crates contain glass bottles, so _____ them "Handle with Care."

13. Her throat was so sore that when she tried to speak all that she could do was

_____ .

Clues Down

1. After you un_____ the horse, you should brush down its coat.

2. Kim Son and her parents moved to the United States from Viet Nam when she was a

_____ of three.

4. Getting a horse used to wearing a _____ takes much time and patience.

6. Mr. and Mrs. Lopez have only one _____, but Mr. and Mrs. Riley next door have four children.

8. The girl ran in a _____ to make it harder for her friend to catch her.

11. You row a boat by taking an _____ in each hand, dipping each in the water, and pulling hard.

WORD LIST 6

ache	icicle	lie
center	igloo	ramble
corner		rim

An **ache** is a dull, steady pain: *The ache in my back went away when I put a warm pad on it.*

To **ache** is to feel a dull, steady pain: *My tooth started to ache, so I called the dentist.*

A **center** is a place where many people go for a special activity: *A new shopping center is opening just outside town.*

The **center** is the place in the exact middle: *A vase of flowers had been put in the center of the table.*

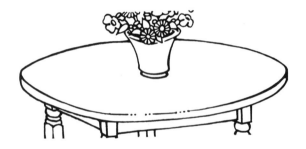

A **corner** is the place where two walls or sides of something meet: *Most rooms have four corners.*

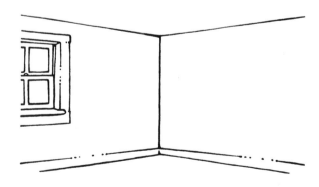

A **corner** is the place where two streets come together: *I will meet you in front of the bookstore at the corner of Eighth Street and University Place.*

To **corner** is to force someone or something into a place that is hard to get out of: *If the dog tries to corner the rat, it will fight to get away.*

An **icicle** is a pointed stick of frozen water that hangs down: *Drops of water running down and freezing form an icicle.*

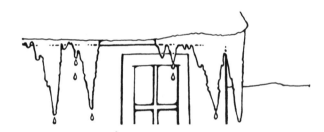

An **igloo** is a small, rounded arctic house made of blocks of hard snow: *An igloo has a hole in the top so that smoke from the fire inside can get out.*

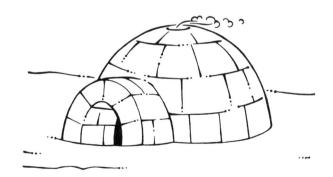

A **lie** is something said or written that is not true: *Jamie says you broke the window, and you say you didn't, so one of you must be telling a lie.*

To **lie** is to say or write something that is not true: *They lie when they say I took the money.*

To **lie** is to be in a flat position: *I like to lie on the grass and look up at the sky.*

To **lie** is to be in a certain place: *Canada lies to the north of the United States.*

To **ramble** is to talk or write at too great a length without sticking closely to the subject: *If the speaker starts to ramble, ask him a question to bring him back to the subject.*

To **ramble** is to walk here and there as one pleases: *We love to ramble in the park looking at the birds and flowers.*

To **ramble** is to grow in all directions: *The roses we have planted will ramble all over the wall.*

A **rim** is the top edge of something round like a bowl or cup: *He filled the cup almost to the rim.*

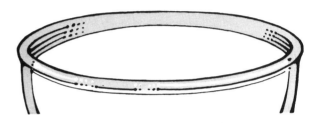

TRUE OR FALSE 6

Some of the sentences below are true and some are false. On the line to the left of each sentence, write *T* if you think the sentence is true, and *F* if you think the sentence is false.

_____ 1. An ache is a dull, steady pain.

_____ 2. An ache is the top edge of something round like a bowl or cup.

_____ 3. The center is the place in the exact middle.

_____ 4. A center is a place where many people go for a special activity.

_____ 5. To corner is to force someone or something into a place that is hard to get out of.

_____ 6. To corner is to talk on and on in an aimless way.

_____ 7. A corner is a place where two walls or sides of something meet.

_____ 8. A corner is the place where two streets come together.

_____ 9. An icicle is a small, rounded arctic house made of blocks of hard snow.

_____ 10. An icicle is a pointed stick of frozen water that hangs down.

_____ 11. An igloo is the top edge of something round like a bowl or cup.

_____ 12. An igloo is a small, rounded arctic house made of blocks of hard snow.

_____ 13. To lie is to be in a flat position.

_____ 14. To lie is to be in a certain place.

_____ 15. To lie is to write or say something that is not true.

_____ 16. To ramble is to grow in all directions.

_____ 17. To ramble is to feel a dull, steady pain.

_____ 18. To ramble is to talk or write at too great a length without sticking closely to the subject.

_____ 19. A rim is the top edge of something round like a cup or bowl.

_____ 20. A rim is a long walk in the woods.

Check your answers against the correct ones below. They are not in order. This is to prevent your eye from catching sight of the correct answers before you have had a chance to do the exercise on your own.

19 T.	13 T.	6 F.	10 T.	1 T.	4 T.	9 F.	15 T.	11 F.	2 F.
3 T.	18 T.	12 T.	8 T.	5 T.	17 F.	7 T.	20 F.	16 T.	14 T.

34

HIDDEN MESSAGE 6

In the boxes next to each definition, write the correct vocabulary word from Word List 6. Put one letter in each box. If you do this properly, the long boxes running from top to bottom will answer the following riddle:

Why did Silly Millie take a hammer and saw upstairs?

1. a place where many people go for a special activity

2. to force someone or something into a place that is hard to get out of

3. the top edge of something round like a bowl or cup

4. to walk here and there as one pleases

5. to say or write something that is not true

6. to grow in all directions

7. a small, rounded arctic house made of blocks of hard snow

8. a pointed stick of frozen water that hangs down

9. the place in the exact middle

10. a dull, steady pain

11. the place where two walls or sides of something meet

12. to talk or write at too great a length without sticking closely to the subject

13. to be in a certain place

k

d

s.

CROSSWORD 6

Decide what word from Word List 6 is missing from each sentence below. For the first group of sentences (Clues Across), write each answer in the boxes running across on the puzzle on the next page. For the second group (Clues Down), write each answer in the boxes running down.

Work out the sentences in any order you like; just be sure to match the number of the sentence with the number in the box. Put only one letter in each box. If all your answers are correct, all the words on the puzzle will fit together.

Clues Across

3. After Tina fell out of the tree, every part of her body seemed to _____.

5. The distance from the surface of the earth to its _____ is 3,950 miles.

7. The glass she used had a red lipstick mark on the _____.

8. The robbers will shoot their way out if the police try to _____ them.

10. I was feeling tired and went to _____ down for a while.

12. I let Mr. Micawber _____ on about his plans for the future without really listening to what he was saying.

15. If you _____ when the judge asks you a question, you can be punished for it.

16. To get to the subway, turn left at the next _____.

Clues Down

1. I still have an _____ in my arm where the ball hit me.

2. The new sports _____ has a swimming pool, a gym, and a running track.

4. The _____ that I broke off melted when I brought it indoors.

5. The baby cried when he bumped his head on the _____ of the table.

6. No one has lived there for years, and vines _____ all over the house and garden.

9. On Sundays when the streets aren't so crowded, we love to _____ around downtown.

11. Although it is made of snow, an _____ is quite warm inside.

13. I told a _____ when I said I had done my homework.

14. Does Mexico _____ to the north or to the south of the United States?

36

WORD LIST 7

badge	knot	shin
comfort	letter	skim
feather	notch	tail

A **badge** is something worn to show that a person belongs to a certain group: *The badge on the police officer's cap had his number on it.*

A **comfort** is anything that makes a sad, sick, or frightened person feel better: *The little girl's teddy bear was a comfort to her in the hospital.*

To **comfort** is to make someone feel less sad: *We tried to comfort the little boy who had lost his dog.*

A **feather** is a part of a bird that grows out from its skin and helps to keep it warm: *The feathers of a duck are oily to keep it from getting wet.*

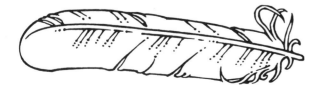

A **knot** is a fastening made by tightly tying something like rope or string that can be looped and pulled on: *Sailors learn to tie many kinds of knots.*

To **knot** is to fasten by tying tightly: *Knot these short pieces of string together to make one long string.*

A **knot** is a hard, dark spot in wood that shows the place where a branch had formed: *Pine boards have many knots in them.*

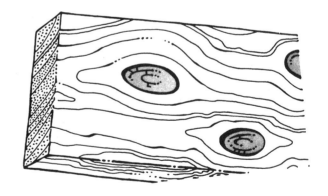

A **letter** is a written or printed message usually put in an envelope and mailed: *Write a letter to Uncle Max thanking him for the gift.*

A **letter** is a written sign that stands for a spoken sound: *"Z" is the last letter of the alphabet.*

A **notch** is a V-shaped cut: *The tent pegs have notches in them so that the ropes holding up the tent won't slip.*

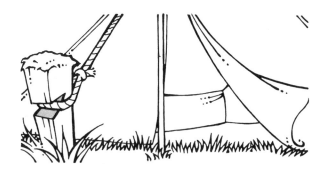

To **shin** is to climb by gripping first with the arms and then with the legs: *She can shin up a rope faster than anyone I know.*

The **shin** is the front part of the leg between the knee and the ankle: *A kick in the shin is very painful.*

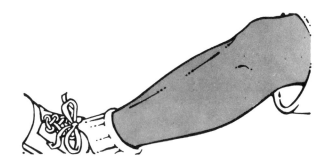

To **skim** is to remove floating matter from the top of a liquid: *Skim the fat from the top of the chicken soup.*

To **skim** is to look over quickly without reading fully: *I skimmed that book you gave me, and I think it looks very interesting.*

The **tail** is the part of an animal's body that sticks out from the back end: *A dog wags its tail when it's happy.*

A **tail** is the part that sticks out from the back of something: *The tail of an airplane helps to keep it steady as it flies.*

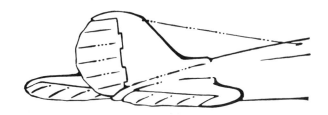

TRUE OR FALSE 7

Some of the sentences below are true and some are false. On the line to the left of each sentence, write *T* if you think the sentence is true, and *F* if you think the sentence is false.

_____ 1. A badge is a V-shaped cut.

_____ 2. A badge is something worn to show that a person belongs to a certain group.

_____ 3. To comfort is to make someone feel less sad.

_____ 4. A comfort is anything that makes a sad, sick, or frightened person feel better.

_____ 5. A feather is a part of a bird that grows out from its skin and helps to keep it warm.

_____ 6. A feather is the part of a car that fits over the engine and that can be raised or lowered.

_____ 7. A knot is a fastening made by tightly tying something like a rope or string that can be looped and pulled on.

_____ 8. A knot is a hard, dark spot in wood that shows the place where a branch had formed.

_____ 9. To knot is to mark an object with a piece of paper or cloth to tell something about it.

_____ 10. A letter is a written sign that stands for a spoken sound.

_____ 11. A letter is a written or printed message usually put in an envelope and mailed.

_____ 12. A notch is the part that sticks out from the back end of something.

_____ 13. A notch is a V-shaped cut.

_____ 14. To shin is to climb by gripping first with the arms and then with the legs.

_____ 15. The shin is the front part of the leg between the knee and the ankle.

_____ 16. To skim is to remove floating matter from the top of a liquid.

_____ 17. To skim is to look over quickly without reading fully.

_____ 18. The tail is the part of an animal's body that sticks out from the back end.

_____ 19. A tail is the part that sticks out from the back of something.

Check your answer against the correct ones below. They are not in order. This is to prevent your eye from catching sight of the correct answers before you have had a chance to do the exercise on your own.

16 T.	2 T.	7 T.	12 F.	10 T.	19 T.	1 F.	8 T.	3 T.	14 T.
17 T.	9 F.	5 T.	11 T.	15 T.	6 F.	13 T.	18 T.	4 T.	

HIDDEN MESSAGE 7

In the boxes next to each definition, write the correct vocabulary word from Word List 7. Put one letter in each box. If you do this properly, the long boxes running from top to bottom will answer the following riddle:

What do you call a cold lemonade on a hot day?

1. the part of an animal's body that sticks out from the back end

2. a written or printed message usually put in an envelope and mailed

3. to climb by gripping first with the arms and then with the legs

4. to remove floating matter from the top of a liquid

5. anything that makes a sad, sick, or frightened person feel better

6. the front part of the leg between the knee and the ankle

7. a written sign that stands for a spoken sound

8. a part of a bird that grows out from its skin and helps to keep it warm

9. to look over quickly without reading fully

10. Something worn to show that a person belongs to a certain group

11. a hard, dark spot in wood that shows the place where a branch had formed

12. the part that sticks out from the back of something

13. a V-shaped cut

CROSSWORD 7

Decide what word from Word List 7 is missing from each sentence below. For the first group of sentences (Clues Across), write each answer in the boxes running across on the puzzle on the next page. For the second group (Clues Down), write each answer in the boxes running down.

Work out the sentences in any order you like; just be sure to match the number of the sentence with the number in the box. Put only one letter in each box. If all your answers are correct, all the words on the puzzle will fit together.

Clues Across

2. The kite's _____ got caught in one of the branches of the tree.

5. Football players wear _____ guards to protect their legs.

6. Inky the cat was a great _____ to Granny when Blackie the dog died.

8. The cow kept swishing its _____ to shoo away the flies.

9. He won a scout _____ for skill in swimming.

11. I offered to _____ up the tree to rescue the kitten.

14. We watched the ball game through a _____ hole in the wooden fence.

15. Nothing we did seemed to _____ the little boy who was lost.

Clues Down

1. Wind one end of the clothesline around the tree and make a _____ to hold it there.

3. The _____ began, "Dear Sir."

4. When you make a rug, you have to _____ each piece of wool tightly in place.

5. I _____ the newspaper in the morning and read it fully in the evening.

7. She seems as light as a _____ when she dances.

10. Always start a sentence with a capital _____.

12. There was a _____ on the post so we could tie up the boat there.

13. _____ the cream off the milk and put it aside.

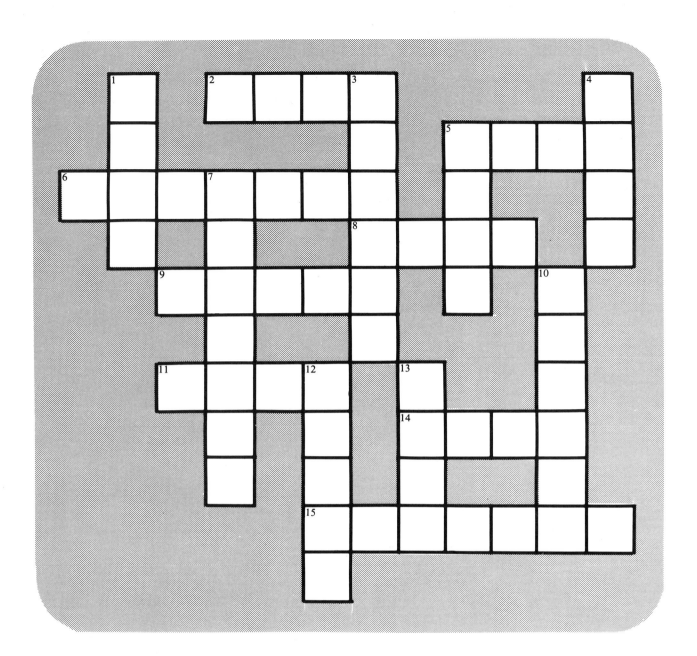

WORD LIST 8

award	churn	errand
boulder	deadly	girder
casual	echo	slogan

An **award** is a prize given for having done well: *She received this book as an award for good work in math.*

To **award** is to give a prize for having done well: *The judges decided to award a prize for the best-trained dog in the pet show.*

A **boulder** is a large rock that has been worn smooth and round because of water and weather: *The train stopped because a boulder had fallen down the mountain and rolled onto the track.*

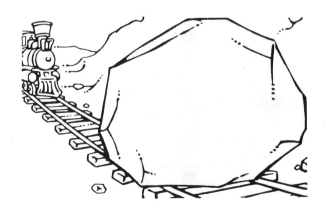

Casual means happening by chance, not planned: *I had a casual visit with the Chu family when I found myself near their house.*

Casual means suitable for wear when there is no need to dress in special clothes: *He wears a suit and tie to work but changes into casual clothes when he gets home.*

A **churn** is a container in which milk or cream is beaten to make butter: *In the old days on the farm, butter was made by hand in a churn.*

To **churn** is to stir up or beat very fast: *The speedboat churned the water as it raced across the lake.*

Deadly means causing death or able to kill: *This poison is so deadly that a single drop can kill you.*

Deadly means very much or extremely: *I tried to read that book but found it deadly dull.*

Deadly means full of hate: *The two families have been deadly enemies for as long as I can remember.*

An **echo** is a sound that bounces back from a surface like a wall so that it is heard twice: *When you shout, you can hear the echo from the side of that tall building.*

To **echo** is to throw back or repeat a sound: *We could hear the sides of the tunnel echo our footsteps as we walked.*

An **errand** is a short trip to do something: *I was on an errand for my mother when I met my friend.*

A **girder** is a long steel or wooden beam used as a support in structures like bridges and buildings: *Seen from its end, the girder has an "H" shape, which gives it extra strength.*

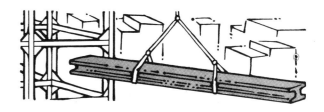

A **slogan** is a word or group of words that is easily remembered and that is used to get people to pay attention: *"Speed Kills" is a slogan used to get people to drive more safely.*

TRUE OR FALSE 8

Some of the sentences below are true and some are false. On the line to the left of each sentence, write _T_ if you think the sentence is true, and _F_ if you think the sentence is false.

_____ 1. An award is a prize given for having done well.

_____ 2. An award is a short trip to do something.

_____ 3. A boulder is a sound that bounces back from a surface like a wall so that it is heard twice.

_____ 4. A boulder is a large rock that has been worn smooth and round because of weather and water.

_____ 5. Casual means suitable for wearing when there is no need to dress in special clothes.

_____ 6. Casual means happening by chance, not planned.

_____ 7. A churn is a container in which milk or cream is beaten to make butter.

_____ 8. To churn is to stir up or beat very fast.

_____ 9. Deadly means causing death or able to kill.

_____ 10. Deadly means very much or extremely.

_____ 11. To echo is to throw back or repeat a sound.

_____ 12. To echo is to give a prize for having done well.

_____ 13. An errand is a word or group of words that is easily remembered and that is used to get people to pay attention.

_____ 14. An errand is a short trip to do something.

_____ 15. A girder is a long steel or wooden beam used as a support in structures like bridges and buildings.

_____ 16. A girder is a large rock that has been worn smooth and round because of weather and water.

_____ 17. A slogan is something that happens by chance.

_____ 18. A slogan is a word or group of words that is easily remembered and that is used to get people to pay attention.

Check your answers against the correct ones below. They are not in order. This is to prevent your eye from catching sight of the correct answers before you have had a chance to do the exercise on your own.

9 T. 12 F. 2 F. 6 T. 18 T. 5 T. 1 T. 11 T. 16 F.
14 T. 7 T. 10 T. 8 T. 3 F. 17 F. 4 T. 13 F. 15 T.

HIDDEN MESSAGE 8

In the boxes next to each definition, write the correct vocabulary word from Word List 8. Put one letter in each box. If you do this properly, the long boxes running from top to bottom will answer the following riddle:

What is the best way to stop growing bald?

1. a word or a group of words that is easily remembered and that is used to get people to pay attention

2. to stir up or beat very fast

3. a large rock that has been worn smooth and round because of water and weather

4. a prize given for having done well

5. suitable for wearing when there is no need to dress in special clothes

6. to throw back or repeat a sound

7. very much or extremely

8. a sound that bounces back from a surface like a wall so that it is heard twice

9. a short trip to do something

10. full of hate

11. a container in which milk or cream is beaten to make butter

12. happening by chance, not planned

13. a long steel or wooden beam used as a support in structures like bridges or buildings

14. to give a prize for having done well

CROSSWORD 8

Decide what word from Word List 8 is missing from each sentence below. For the first group of sentences (Clues Across), write each answer in the boxes running across on the puzzle on the next page. For the second group (Clues Down), write each answer in the boxes running down.

Work out the sentences in any order you like; just be sure to match the number of the sentence with the number in the box. Put only one letter in each box. If all your answers are correct, all the words on the puzzle will fit together.

Clues Across

1. I had a _____ meeting with the school principal when we met in the school parking lot.

5. "Hello!" she shouted into the cave, and "Hello!" came back the _____.

7. Each _____ is bolted into place to make the frame of the skyscraper.

9. This paddle is used to _____ the cream into butter.

11. The four of us pushed with all our strength, but we could not roll the _____ out of the way.

13. The soldier was thrilled when he was told that the president would _____ him the medal he had won.

15. Doctors can now cure many diseases once thought _____.

Clues Down

2. "Sweet Dreams" is the _____ of a company that makes beds.

3. This small silver cup was her first _____ for roller skating.

4. After it has been used to make butter, the _____ should be carefully washed out and rinsed.

6. The invitation to the party said "_____ dress," so I wore a sweater and jeans.

8. As he lay in pain, he could hear his calls for help _____ off the side of the mountain.

10. The man in the apartment across the hall gave me a dollar to run an _____ for him.

12. She was _____ serious when she said I was getting my last chance.

14. The _____ quarrel between the two men lasted for many years.

49

branch	chest	ruler
brooch	crack	soak
brush	cry	stare

A **branch** is a part of a tree that grows out from the trunk: *You have to climb up the trunk of the tree to reach the branches.*

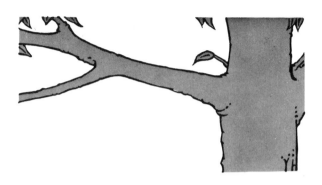

A **branch** is a part of something that is away from the main part: *Besides the main library, there are six branch libraries in this city.*

To **branch** is to split or divide into two or more parts: *To get to the lake, you go left where the road branches up ahead.*

A **brooch** is a pin used to decorate one's clothing: *She wore the brooch that had been given to her by her grandmother.*

A **brush** is an object made of short, stiff hair or wire fastened to a handle: *A wire brush was used to remove dirt and loose paint from the outside of the house.*

To **brush** is to clean, put on paint, or arrange hair with a brush: *Brush your teeth before you go to bed.*

Brush is bushes and small trees growing close together: *The land where we cut down the trees last year is now covered with brush.*

A **chest** is a heavy box fitted with a lid: *The pirate chief kept his gold locked in a chest.*

The **chest** is the upper part of the body between the stomach and the neck: *The heart and lungs are inside the chest.*

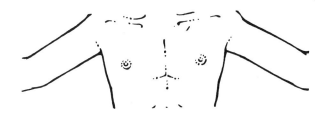

A **crack** is a break in something where the parts still hold together: *He served my coffee in a cup with a large crack in it.*

A **crack** is a sudden, sharp noise: *The crack of the whip made the horse jump.*

To **crack** is to split or break open: *I watched him crack the nuts with his teeth.*

A **cry** is a loud noise made by a person or some kinds of animals: *I lay on the beach and listened to the cry of a gull far above me.*

To **cry** is to make a loud noise with the voice: *I heard her cry out in pain when she fell and broke her leg.*

To **cry** is to shed tears or to weep: *She tried not to cry when she heard the bad news.*

A **ruler** is a straight strip of wood, plastic, or metal that is marked off in inches and used for measuring: *You can use your ruler to draw a straight line.*

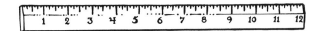

A **ruler** is a person who runs a country and decides what needs to be done for it: *Elizabeth I, queen of England, was ruler of that country for forty-five years.*

To **soak** is to keep something in water or other liquid for a long time: *You should let the dirty clothes soak for a while before washing them.*

To **stare** is to look at something for a long time without moving the eyes: *It is not polite to stare at a person who is in some way different from others.*

TRUE OR FALSE 9

Some of the sentences below are true and some are false. On the line to the left of each sentence, write *T* if you think the sentence is true, and *F* if you think the sentence is false.

_____ 1. A branch is a part of a tree that grows out from the trunk.

_____ 2. A branch is a part of something that is away from the main part.

_____ 3. A brooch is a heavy box fitted with a lid.

_____ 4. A brooch is a pin used to decorate one's clothing.

_____ 5. A brush is an object made of short, stiff hair or wire fastened to a handle.

_____ 6. Brush is bushes and small trees growing close together.

_____ 7. The chest is the upper part of the body between the stomach and the neck.

_____ 8. A chest is a heavy box fitted with a lid.

_____ 9. A crack is a sudden, sharp noise.

_____ 10. A crack is a sound that bounces back from a surface so that is is heard twice.

_____ 11. A crack is a break in something where the parts still hold together.

_____ 12. To cry is to make a loud noise with the voice.

_____ 13. To cry is to shed tears or to weep.

_____ 14. A ruler is a person who runs a country and decides what needs to be done for it.

_____ 15. A ruler is a straight strip of wood, plastic, or metal that is marked off in inches and used for measuring.

_____ 16. To soak is to split or divide into two or more parts.

_____ 17. To soak is to keep something in water or other liquid for a long time.

_____ 18. To stare is to split or break open.

_____ 19. To stare is to look at something for a long time without moving the eyes.

Check your answers against the correct ones below. They are not in order. This is to prevent your eye from catching sight of the correct answers before you have had a chance to do the exercise on your own.

10 F. 14 T. 11 T. 1 T. 8 T. 18 F. 2 T. 5 T. 13 T. 19 T.
3 F. 9 T. 6 T. 17 T. 12 T. 4 T. 15 T. 7 T. 16 F.

HIDDEN MESSAGE 9

In the boxes next to each definition, write the correct vocabulary word from Word List 9. Put one letter in each box. If you do this properly, the long boxes running from top to bottom will answer the following riddle:

Which burns longer, a fat candle or a thin candle?

1. to split or divide into two or more parts

2. a pin used to decorate one's clothing

3. to look at for a long time without moving the eyes

4. bushes and small trees growing close together

5. a part of something that is away from the main part

6. a person who runs a country and decides what needs to be done for it

7. a break in something where the parts still hold together

8. a part of a tree that grows out from the trunk

9. an object made of short, stiff hair or wire fastened to a handle

10. the upper part of the body between the stomach and the neck

11. to keep something in water or other liquid for a long time

12. a loud noise made by a person or some kinds of animals

13. a heavy box fitted with a lid

14. a straight strip of wood, plastic, or metal that is marked off in inches and used for measuring

15. to split or break open

CROSSWORD 9

Decide what word from Word List 9 is missing from each sentence below. For the first group of sentences (Clues Across), write each answer in the boxes running across on the puzzle on the next page. For the second group (Clues Down), write each answer in the boxes running down.

Work out the sentences in any order you like; just be sure to match the number of the sentence with the number in the box. Put only one letter in each box. If all your answers are correct, all the words on the puzzle will fit together.

Clues Across

1. The swing was tied to a high _____ of the old elm tree.

5. I thought I heard someone _____ for help.

6. The doctor learns a great deal about your health by listening to the sounds in your _____.

7. The _____ of a rifle broke the silence.

11. Mrs. Travis ran the _____ office of the bank before she moved to the main office.

12. We are going to build our own house, but first we must clear the lot of all the _____.

13. My feet were so sore from running that I just wanted to _____ them in cool water after the race.

14. She could only _____ at me in amazement when I told her she had won a thousand dollars.

15. We heard the _____ of the lost lamb, but we could not see it.

17. _____ the cobwebs off the ceiling, and dust the tables and chairs.

Clues Down

2. It is better when people of a country choose their own _____.

3. Seagulls _____ open the clams by dropping them on rocks.

4. Use this _____ to clean your fingernails.

8. Fill in that _____ in the ceiling with plaster.

9. Put the hammer back in the tool _____ when you have finished with it.

10. Draw a line six inches long with your _____.

11. Fasten the _____ properly, or it will come loose and fall off.

12. The trunk of a pine tree does not _____ but grows straight up.

16. I bet the sad movie will make you _____.

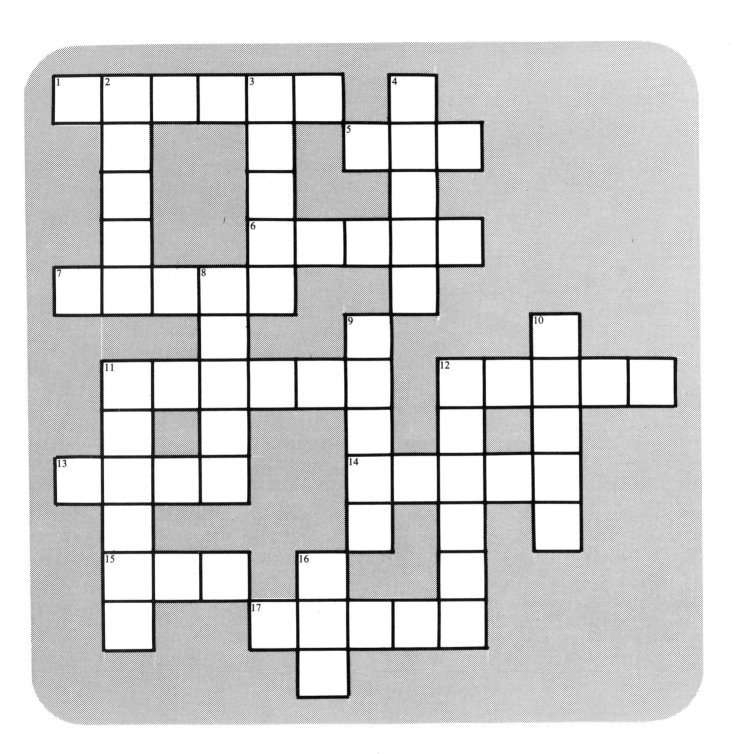

WORD LIST 10

angle	cradle	fang
beach	embroider	frigid
cereal		lean

An **angle** is the shape made by two straight lines meeting at a point: *The size of an angle is given in degrees, as shown in the figures below.*

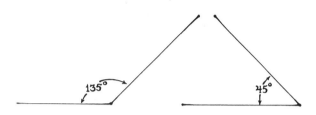

An **angle** is a way of looking at something: *Fumiko took pictures of the house from every angle.*

To **angle** is to fish with a hook and line: *He went on a fishing trip with some friends who also like to angle.*

A **beach** is a strip of sand or pebbles at the edge of a sea or other large body of water: *This beach is a good place to look for seashells.*

To **beach** is to move from the water onto the shore: *Sometimes whales swim too close to the shore and beach themselves.*

A **cereal** is a plant whose seed or grain is used as a food: *Corn and barley are cereals.*

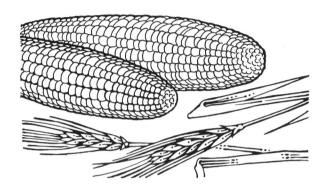

A **cereal** is a breakfast food made from certain kinds of grain: *Cornflakes and oatmeal are popular cereals.*

A **cradle** is a small baby's bed that can be gently rocked: *The baby stopped crying and fell asleep when I rocked her in the cradle.*

To **cradle** is to hold gently in the arms: *Father cradled the little boy in his arms.*

To **embroider** is to make designs on cloth with a needle and thread: *She has started to embroider the hem of her skirt.*

A **fang** is a sharp, hollow tooth through which some snakes shoot poison: *The rattlesnake has two fangs in its upper jaw.*

56

A **fang** is a long, pointed tooth that an animal such as a wolf or lion uses to tear apart meat for food: *The dog's fangs were about to close on the rabbit when it escaped down its hole.*

Frigid means very cold: *The air was frigid in the room where the meat was kept in cold storage.*

Lean means without fat: *The greyhound is a lean animal that can run very fast.*

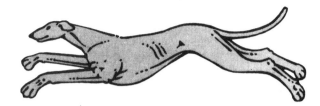

Lean means poor or without much money: *The ski resorts had a lean season because there was not much snow.*

To **lean** is to slant to one side: *The famous Tower of Pisa in Italy leans quite a bit to one side.*

TRUE OR FALSE 10

Some of the sentences below are true and some are false. On the line to the left of each sentence, write *T* if you think the sentence is true, and *F* if you think the sentence is false.

_____ 1. An angle is the shape made by two straight lines meeting at a point.

_____ 2. An angle is a way of looking at something.

_____ 3. To angle is to make designs on cloth with a needle and thread.

_____ 4. To angle is to fish with a hook and line.

_____ 5. A beach is a strip of sand or pebbles at the edge of the sea or other large body of water.

_____ 6. To beach is to move from the water onto the shore.

_____ 7. A cereal is a breakfast food made from certain kinds of grain.

_____ 8. A cereal is a plant whose seed or grain is used as a food.

_____ 9. To cradle is to hold gently in the arms.

_____ 10. A cradle is a small baby's bed that can be gently rocked.

_____ 11. A cradle is a box fitted with a lid.

_____ 12. To embroider is to fish with a hook and line.

_____ 13. To embroider is to make designs on cloth with a needle and thread.

_____ 14. A fang is a long, pointed tooth that an animal such as a wolf or lion uses to tear apart meat for food.

_____ 15. A fang is a sharp, hollow tooth through which some snakes shoot poison.

_____ 16. Frigid means full of hate.

_____ 17. Frigid means very cold.

_____ 18. Lean means without fat.

_____ 19. Lean means poor or without much money.

_____ 20. To lean is to slant to one side.

Check your answers against the correct ones below. They are not in order. This is to prevent your eye from catching sight of the correct answers before you have had a chance to do the exercise on your own.

| 5 F. | 18 T. | 11 F. | 15 T. | 1 T. | 7 T. | 14 T. | 20 T. | 12 F. | 2 T. |
| 9 T. | 3 F. | 10 T. | 19 T. | 13 T. | 4 T. | 16 F. | 6 T. | 17 T. | 8 T. |

HIDDEN MESSAGE 10

In the boxes next to each definition, write the correct vocabulary word from Word List 10. Put one letter in each box. If you do this properly, the long boxes running from top to bottom will answer the following riddle:

Why did Silly Millie spill the glass of water?

1. to make designs on cloth with a needle and thread

2. a strip of sand or pebbles at the edge of a sea or other large body of water

3. the shape made by two straight lines meeting at a point

4. to move from the water onto the shore

5. to slant to one side

6. without fat

7. a plant whose seed or grain is used as a food

8. very cold

9. a sharp, hollow tooth through which some snakes shoot poison

10. a breakfast food made from certain kinds of grain

11. to fish with a hook and line

12. to hold gently in the arms

CROSSWORD 10

Decide what word from Word List 10 is missing from each sentence below. For the first group of sentences (Clues Across), write each answer in the boxes running across on the puzzle on the next page. For the second group (Clues Down), write each answer in the boxes running down.

Work out the sentences in any order you like; just be sure to match the number of the sentence with the number in the box. Put only one letter in each box. If all your answers are correct, all the words on the puzzle will fit together.

Clues Across

5. He sucked the poison from the hole made by the snake's _____, and then he carefully spat it out.

6. Sugar-coated _____ is not good for your teeth.

7. It took Tanya three months to _____ the edges of this tablecloth with these colorful flowers.

11. A _____ such as wheat grows well in this colder part of the state.

13. We carefully studied the problem from every _____.

15. She had to _____ forward so she could hear better.

16. Each _____ of a square is the same shape as the other three.

Clues Down

1. We have to _____ the boat so that we can scrape and paint the bottom.

2. The _____ that the infant sleeps in is over a hundred years old.

3. She loves to _____ and once caught a fifteen-pound trout.

4. It was on a _____ day in January that the oil furnace broke down.

8. We raced down the _____ and ran splashing into the waves.

9. We let Judy pick up the sick puppy and _____ it in her arms.

10. Animals such as cows and sheep have no _____ like teeth because they eat only grass.

12. The 1930s were _____ years for most people in the United States because so many were out of work at that time.

14. To make the stew, you first cut up a pound of _____ beef.